1 John

A Study of the Apostle John's First Epistle to the Followers of Christ

Miriam Hamstra

Copyright © 2017 Miriam Hamstra

The right of Miriam Hamstra to be identified as the author of the work has been asserted by him in accordance with the Copyright, Designs, and Patents Act 1998.

All rights reserved. No part of this publication may be reproduced, stored in a retrieval system, or transmitted in any form by any means, electronically, mechanical, photocopy, recording, or otherwise, without prior permission of the author, except as provided for by the USA copyright law.

This book is sold subject to the condition that it shall not, by any way of trade or otherwise, without the author's prior consent in any form.

ISBN-10: 1979928088
ISBN-13: 978-1979928083

DEDICATION

My parents: who taught me of the love of the Savior and who encourage me to press on in the faith when it is easy and even when it hurts.

My sister: my dearest friend and the one with whom I share life's high and lows, who motivates me to trust God daily. She encourages me to seek God's will in all circumstance of life.

My mentor: my constant encourager, who has taught me to study the Word in a deeper way. She faithfully ensures I am walking in step with what I say I believe.

You four are gifts from God, and I thank Him for you.

CONTENTS

Chapter 1   1

Chapter 2   12

Chapter 3   28

Chapter 4   38

Chapter 5   48

Foreward

My desire for this book is that we see and learn what God wants for us to see. The theme of 1 John is love. John shows believers in Christ that the quality of our love and whom we love is important. In fact, it is so important that it is a defining characteristic of a living faith. Are you loving others? What is your first love? If it is not God, who is it? What does your love life look like with others? Is there any love for them, or is it hatred? These questions are going to be answered by John to show what true love looks like.

One of the reasons why I love the book of 1 John is because it is a book that we can always learn from. It is a book that speaks to anyone at any area of life. It is also a great book for the new believer because it speaks practical truths that any Christian will learn from. We will look at the question, "What does it mean for me to be a follower of Christ?"

John wants believers who may not be new to the faith to apply these practical truths to our lives. John wrote this book not because we do not know the truth, but because we do! It is a book that reminds us of the duties of the Christian. It shows what a living faith looks like. It also serves as the constant reminder that we need the truth ever before us even if we think we have heard it so many times. We are not to grow old of the faith. The goal of this book is to look at the truths of God's Word and ask, "Are these truths and qualities in me?" You will see often throughout the book this phrase or similar ones, "By this we know…" John shows clearly what the fruits of a Christian are to be. These works don't save us, but they are clear markers of genuine faith.

God also desires that you be reminded of the truth, but that you don't just stop there. We are all commanded to take these commands and obey them and therefore live lives of thankfulness for the great love that has been bestowed upon us. I hope your study of 1 John will show you why that love is so important and equip you to take the love of Christ that is in you to those we come in contact with.

As you read through 1 John, examine your life. Are you living rightly? John will be showing a lot of proof of a genuine faith. Be asking yourself if it is in you.

I have chosen to use the NKJV version of the Bible. My prayer is that you are blessed by this study and that the study of this portion of God's Word proves beneficial and changes you as it has changed me!

In Christ,
Miriam Hamstra.

The First Epistle of John

Chapter 1

The Apostle John

The writer of 1 John is the apostle John. He was a direct apostle of Jesus Christ and witnessed Christ's life, death, resurrection and ascension. Although John doesn't introduce himself, these writings are very similar to his other books. He wrote three other books: Second and Third John and Revelation, which he wrote on the island of Patmos. John's style of writing gets right into doctrine. He often does not introduce himself and starts out the gospel of John and this book, 1 John, by declaring Christ. John is eager for others to know Christ. He, being an eyewitness of Christ, is not shy in declaring who Christ is despite what others think. We will look at this more later. We will be often referring back to the gospel of John which ties in to what John is seeking to teach the believers of Christ.

The Eyewitness Testimony from the Apostles

John starts out his letter of 1 John by characterizing the Word which is where we will start our study as well. My goal for us is to see what the apostle John says about the Word. John gets right to it and says in verse 1, "That which was from the beginning, which we have heard, which we have seen with our eyes, which we have looked upon, and our hands have handled, concerning the Word of life." The Word is from the beginning. John is showing his authenticity to his knowledge of Christ. He is bearing witness to what was seen, heard and touched. People often denied these apostles' accounts, but John tells his readers that he saw Christ with his eyes and had touched Him. These twelve disciples knew Christ. They really knew Him because they spent three years following him and learning from Him. They knew who He was. They knew what He loved. They saw Jesus' miracles, heard his teaching, and even saw Him being taken away by the soldiers to be scourged and killed. They saw Christ all the way to His ascension. These apostles were the first of Christ's church and received the Holy Spirit when Christ ascended into heaven. John is giving a true account of the doctrine (teaching) of Christ and is giving an accurate report of Christ because he knew Christ personally. These disciples knew Christ well and now John shares more of the teachings of Christ through this first epistle. These are truths from a eyewitness of Jesus Christ.

Before we begin, I want to look at three aspects of Jesus. This will help us understand who this Jesus is that John will be testifying to throughout his epistle.

Jesus the Word of God

John, despite what others have said, wants his readers to know that Jesus is the Word. Jesus is God. This means that what Christ says is equal to what God says because what Christ says is what the Father has said. Look at John 5:19,

"Then Jesus answered and said to them, 'Most assuredly, I say to you, the Son can do nothing of Himself, but what He sees the Father do; for whatever He does, the Son also does in like manner.'"

The Son does what the Father does. If the Son does or says something, it is because the Father did it or said it. So with all that is said, Jesus is God's Word. This isn't the first time the apostle John has said this. Look at John 1:1.

"In the beginning was the Word, and the Word was with God, and the Word was God."

The Word, who is God was in the beginning. Although Genesis does not come right out and say Christ is in the creation, He was. John 1:2 says,

"He was in the beginning with God."

He was there orchestrating with the Father the creation of the world. Jesus Christ, who gave Himself for us, has been since the foundation of the world. We have an Omnipotent Savior who knows everything, has never had a beginning or and an end, and is eternal. Because Christ is God's Word, we can know that the Bible is reliable. It is trustworthy and God-breathed.

How Jesus Relates in Comparison to the Word of God

The Word shows us ourselves and who we really are. It discerns the heart and its intentions. It is the standard for our lives. Hebrews 4:12 says,

"For the word of God is living and powerful, and sharper than any two-edged sword, piercing even to the division of soul and spirit, and of joints and marrow, and is a discerner of the thoughts and intents of the heart."

The Word shows us what we do and why we act the way we do. It does this with power. The Word is living and active. When we read it, learn from it, and take it to heart, the Word pierces us and changes us. That is a good thing because we need to be more like Christ. The Word shows us our sin, but it also shows us our Savior.

We must know the Word well so we will know how to discern between godly and evil voices. We need to know the Good Shepherd's voice. Knowing our Shepherd's voice will keep us from sin. John 10:3-5 says,

> *"To him the doorkeeper opens, and the sheep hear his voice; and he calls his own sheep by name and leads them out. And when he brings out his own sheep, he goes before them; and the sheep follow him, for they know his voice. Yet they will by no means follow a stranger, but will flee from him, for they do not know the voice of strangers."*

We need to know the Word so that we will be able to run from false teachers. We will be firm and know that our shepherd's voice is our guide. We cannot follow a shepherd if we do not know Him well. After we know this Word and this voice well, we will start seeing how following the Shepherd changes us. Those who do not spend time learning their Shepherd will not be able to recognize His voice.

When we know the Word and are living by it, we will not sin. Psalm 119:11 says,

> *"I have stored up your word in my heart, that I might not sin against you."*

That is because when we follow the shepherd, and those who follow him fully will not go astray. The same is with us. If we are studying the Word and desiring to know more, we will not go astray looking for a more entertaining way. This is the way of the world. We have the Way. We have the Truth and the Life. Jesus, our Word, is all we need. We need to study and learn our Shepherd's voice. We recognize Him by His Words. They are found here in the Word. The Bible and Jesus never contradict one another. If we want to be able to know the truth and avoid the false teachings, then we need to know the Word and follow our Shepherd's voice. John wants us to know this Word like he did. He wants us to follow Christ as he did. "That which was from the beginning, which we have heard, which we have seen with our eyes, which we have looked upon, and our hands have handled, concerning the Word of life." The disciples witnessed Christ with their eyes. They touched Him and heard Him talk, but we also have a unique privilege of hearing Christ in His Word. Hebrews 1:1, 2 speaks of this privilege,

> *"God, who at various times and in various ways spoke in time past to the fathers by the prophets, has in these last days spoken to us by His Son, whom He has appointed heir of all things, through whom also He made the worlds."*

1. Who is John referring to in verse 1?

2. Who is the Word of Life?

3. How does the Word correspond with Jesus Christ? (John 1:1)

4. Why can we know the Bible is reliable?

5. What two things does the Word of God show us?

6. Why must we know God's Word well?

7. What example does John 10:3-5 give us about knowing God's Word?

Jesus the Son and our Redemption

Jesus lived to declare the Lord's will for redemption. He was born of a virgin which was a miracle. Mary rejoiced and saw the Lord's redemption plan. In Luke 1:46-49 she sings,

"My soul magnifies the Lord, and my spirit rejoices in God my Savior, for he has looked on the humble estate of his servant. For behold, from now on all generations will call me blessed; for he who is mighty has done great things for me, and holy is his name."

From the time the angel brought her the news, she glorified God and remembered the Lord's covenant to His people. She knew that her Son was the Son of God. She knew He came to fulfill the law, but she didn't understand fully. At the age of twelve, Jesus was listening in and answering the questions of the teachers. Luke 2:46-49 recounts,

"Now so it was that after three days they found Him in the temple, sitting in the midst of the teachers, both listening to them and asking them questions. And all who heard Him were astonished at His understanding and answers. So when they saw Him, they were amazed; and His mother said to Him, 'Son, why have You done this to us? Look, Your father and I have sought You anxiously.' And He said to them, 'Why did you seek Me? Did you not know that I must be about My Father's business?'"

This did not make sense to His parents, but Jesus from a young age was declaring and doing the will of His Father. He did not come to do His own will, but was solely focused on the Lord's will. Jesus continued to live a life that was without reproach and even when He was questioned and mocked, He did not sin. He lived His life as a servant. We have been given an example of servanthood. John 13:15 says,

"For I have given you an example, that you should do as I have done to you."

We have an example of how we should live, in service of others. Let us, no matter the circumstance, seek to be servants to others. Christ's life is one of ultimate sacrifice. He laid down His life to redeem His people back to the Father. He was and is the only One who reconciled sinners to God.

1. What did the life of Jesus declare since He was born?

2. Give three ways His life gave testimony to redemption.

3. How does Christ's life give an example for us to follow?

4. Why is a servant's heart important?

5. How can you serve others who cross your path every day?

How Joy Made is Full by Knowing The Word and the Son

John knows that belonging to Christ is when we receive joy. He wrote this book so that we may find joy and that it may be complete. Fellowship with God brings us joy and we find that joy is complete when we are living in fellowship with Him. But what does it mean to have fellowship with God? Well, fellowship according to the dictionary means, "Friendly association, especially with people who share one's interests." This means then that when we are in fellowship with God, we are at peace with Him. We are not blocked by our sins from coming to Him. Because of Christ we are now able to come to Him in peace and have fellowship with Him by praying and reading His Word. Consider Hebrews 10:22,

"Let us draw near with a true heart in full assurance of faith, having our hearts sprinkled from an evil conscience and our bodies washed with pure water."

Since we are washed from our sins, we can now draw near and have fellowship with God. How wonderful! Because of Christ's perfect life, death, and resurrection we now have true peace and fellowship with God.

1. What does it mean to have joy?

2. How do we receive joy according to John?

3. What does it mean to have a joy that is complete?

4. Can we find lasting joy in anything else besides knowing God and being in fellowship with Him?

5. How do we have fellowship with God?

6. What special privilege do we have because of Christ according to Hebrews 10:22?

7. Do you have fellowship with God? If not, what is hindering you from having it?

Fellowship with God and Fellow Christians

Before we can have fellowship with God, we must realize that He is light and that in Him there is no darkness. So, if we are walking in darkness we cannot have fellowship with Him. Look at verse 6 of our passage, "If we say that we have fellowship with Him, and walk in darkness, we lie and do not practice the truth." If we say we are in fellowship yet are living as the world does, in sin, we are deceiving ourselves and we are not practicing the truth. But verse 7 says, "But if we walk in the light as He is in the light, we have fellowship with one another, and the blood of Jesus Christ His Son cleanses us from all sin." So if we are at peace with God, and walking in the light, then we are in fellowship with other

Christians and the blood of Jesus Christ has washed us from our sins. When we sin, we must repent and strive to continue walking in the light. When we repent, God gives us grace to keep doing the right thing. But if we don't repent, verse 8 says, "If we say that we have no sin, we deceive ourselves, and the truth is not in us."
Pride in our lives causes us to be blinded to our sin. Therefore we will say we are without sin and we will be deceiving ourselves and the Truth, the Light, is not in us. Pride will block us from not being able to see our sin. Let us avoid doing what verse 10 says, "If we say that we have not sinned, we make Him a liar, and His word is not in us." God takes sin very seriously. Let us pray and ask God to show us our sin and repent of it. Take comfort in what He says in verse 9 for those who repent. "If we confess our sins, He is faithful and just to forgive us our sins and to cleanse us from all unrighteousness."

1. Before we can have fellowship with God, what must we realize?

2. Can we be in fellowship with the world and God?

3. When are we at true fellowship with God and other Christians?

4. What does it mean to walk in the light?

5. Are you walking in the light as He is in the Light?

6. When does God forgive sins?

7. What are we doing to ourselves if we say we have no sin in our lives?

8. Why is self-deception so serious?

9. Do those who are deceiving themselves have any truth in them? Do they understand God's truth?

10. If we confess our sins, will God forgive them?

11. God forgives us our sin and _____ us from all _____.

12. How does this comfort you as a Christian?

Chapter 2

Why do We Read the Word?

With all that has been said about the Word and how John shows Jesus is the Word, I think that it is a good idea that we focus on why we should be studying these things. John says in 2:1a "My little children, these things I write to you, so that you may not sin." John writes these things so that we may know the truth and that we may not sin. Psalm 119:11 says about the Word of God,

"Your word I have hidden in my heart, That I might not sin against You."

We must store up the Word in our hearts so that we may not sin. When we know the Word and use the Sword of the Spirit, which is the Word of God, we will be able to resist temptation from sin. Satan hates the Word, and flees and runs from the Word because it is dangerous to him. Knowing the Word will keep us near to our Shepherd and far from danger of sin. Since we are human, we will sin, and John knows that, so he reminds us that when we sin we, because of Christ's blood now have an Advocate. Our Savior is our advocate when we sin. Look at verse 2 "And He Himself is the propitiation for our sins, and not for ours only but also for the whole world." Christ now intercedes for us and we know have peace with God. What a wonderful promise!

"But where sin abounded, grace abounded much more, so that as sin reigned in death, even so grace might reign through righteousness to eternal life through Jesus Christ our Lord." (Romans 5:20b-21)

When we sin, we are given grace time and time again. We have been given the gift of eternal life by grace through faith.

1. Why did John write this letter to these Christians?

2. How would writing a letter help someone avoid falling into sin?

3. Look up Psalm 119:11. What reason does the psalmist give for memorizing Scripture?

4. How does this method help? Think of when Jesus was tempted by Satan in the wilderness.

5. Is there hope for Christians who sin? What is that hope?

6. Christ was the p_____ for our sins.

7. What does the world mean at the end of verse 2?

How We Know if We Know Him

Verse 3 says because John lays it out plain how we know Him. "Now by this we know that we know Him, if we keep His commandments." There should be no doubt whether we truly know

God. If we keep His commandments, than we *know* that we know God. It is not complicated. It is not confusing. So if we are not obeying God's commandments, we have no right to say we know God. This lines up well with what James says in James 2:26,

> *"For as the body without the spirit is dead, so faith without works is dead also."*

If faith in knowing God is present, then we will be obeying God's commandments. The good works will be there as well. Look what John says in verse 4, "He who says, 'I know Him,' and does not keep His commandments, is a liar, and the truth is not in him." If we are just claiming to have faith, or just saying that we have faith, we are liars and the truth is not in us. If we are liars there is no truth in us. Notice what John says in verse 5, "But whoever keeps His word, truly the love of God is perfected in him. By this we know that we are in Him." The love of God is made complete in those who love God. If we obey God then His love is in us, and we know that we are in Him. If we are in Him and living according to His law, then we must walk as He walked. We must do what He did. Verse 6 says this, "He who says he abides in Him ought himself also to walk just as He walked." We need to be servants as Christ is a servant. Look at John 13:15,

> *"For I have given you an example, that you should do as I have done to you."*

Christ said this after washing the disciples feet. He "stepped down" from being the master and did what a servant did. This isn't a new commandment to us. Look at verse 7, "Brethren, I write no new commandment to you, but an old commandment which you have had from the beginning. The old commandment is the word which you heard from the beginning." Jesus gave us this command. But John does write a new command to those who have Christ in them. John says this in verse 8, "Again, a new commandment I write to you, which thing is true in Him and in you, because the darkness is passing away, and the true light is already shining." Because the darkness of sin is passing away in us and the true light of Christ is shining in us, this new command is for us. Let's see what it is. "He who says he is in the light, and hates his brother, is in darkness until now. He who loves his brother abides in the light, and there is no cause for stumbling in him. But he who hates his brother is in darkness and walks in darkness, and does not know where he is going, because the darkness has blinded his eyes." (1 John 2:9-11) For us to be in the light, we must love our brothers. We must not be trying to live in light while hating our brothers and sisters. It's interesting how John says that those who are loving their brothers have no cause for stumbling because the light is abiding in them. There is no cause for us to fall away because we have the Light in us and we can see where we are going. This is unlike the man who hates his brother. Those who have hate in them are in darkness and therefore cannot see where they are going. Those people are blinded by the darkness and are now at danger for stumbling. Let us be those who are walking faithfully in the light.

1. How do we know if we truly love God?

2. Who is someone who says he loves God but lives like the world?

3. If we want to abide in Christ, what must we do according to verse 6?

4. Examine your life. Do you truly know God? Are you living out His commands?

5. Are you walking after the example of Christ? In what aspect of Christ's life do you need to become more like Him?

6. What is a second way we can know if we are walking in the light?

7. How does this prove a genuine faith?

8. Will a person who loves his brother stumble? Why or why not?

9. Do those who hate their brothers and sisters have a sure step in front of them? Why or why not?

10. Do you love your siblings in your family and in God's family?

11. Do you desire to love them more and more?

12. After you read Galatians 6:10, reflect on how can you love those who are in God's family today.

13. What three age groups is John writing to in this part of the letter?

14. What specific things need to be learned before moving onto more difficult spiritual issues?

15. How do you become a strong Christian like the one in the last part of verse 14?

16. Do you know the understand the Gospel? Would you be able to explain it to someone else? What stage of spiritual maturity are you in right now?

Do Not Love the World

Next is a topic that is very important and something that separates us from the rest of the world. These next verses are very weighty. "Do not love the world or the things in the world. If anyone loves the world, the love of the Father is not in him. For all that is in the world—the lust of the flesh, the lust of the eyes, and the pride of life—is not of the Father but is of the world. And the world is passing away, and the lust of it; but he who does the will of God abides forever." (v.15-17) We are not to love the passions of the world. Colossians 3:8-9 says,

"But now you yourselves are to put off all these: anger, wrath, malice, blasphemy, filthy language out of your mouth. Do not lie to one another, since you have put off the old man with his deeds."

    These deeds are of the old man who is of the world. The Lord calls us to not only abstain from doing what the world does, but we are to hate what it does. What are these things of the world? "For all that is in the world—the lust of the flesh, the lust of the eyes, and the pride of life—is not of the Father but is of the world." The world thinks that if we are drunk and gluttonous, (lust of the flesh), coveting others' possessions (lust of the eyes), and proud in ourselves and our abilities (pride of life) - then we will be happy. But those who live like that are not of the Father. They are of the world and consumed by the filth in it. John gives us a reason why we are not to be consumed by the customs of the world, and why we are to say "no" to the world. Look at verse 17, "And the world is passing away, and the lust of it; but he who does the will of God abides forever." The world isn't going to be here forever. The "satisfaction" of being drunk and the pleasures of other's things doesn't truly satisfy us. It is going to pass away and mean nothing. But He who obeys the commands and will of God will abide forever. You may be wondering why we can't love God and the things of the world at the same time. Take a look at how Paul says it in Romans 8:7-8.

"Because the carnal mind is enmity against God; for it is not subject to the law of God, nor indeed can be. So then, those who are in the flesh cannot please God."

    Those who are in the flesh are enemies of God. We can't serve both. We can't be on both sides. Jesus said in Matthew 6:24,

"No one can serve two masters; for either he will hate the one and love the other, or else he will be loyal to the one and despise the other. You cannot serve God and mammon."

Mammon comes from the Aramaic word *māmōn* which means riches. The riches of the world. The world is an enemy of God. We cannot serve both. Let us serve God alone.

"You shall have no other gods before Me." Exodus 20:3

1. What two things are we not to love according to verse 15?

2. What does it mean to love the world?

3. Can you love God and the world? (v. 15, Matthew 6:24)

4. What three things are in the world?

5. What is the lust of the flesh?

6. What is the lust of the eye?

7. What is the pride of life?

8. Do these lusts and passions come from God? Where do they come from?

9. Why are we to abide in God?

10. Are you doing the will of God?

The Last Hour

I love how John says it in verse 18, "Little children, it is the last hour; and as you have heard that the Antichrist is coming, even now many antichrists have come, by which we know that it is the last hour." We are in the last hour right now and we know this by knowing that antichrists have come and there is one coming. We need to be faithful. Jesus says this in Matthew 24:24,

> *"For false christs and false prophets will rise and show great signs and wonders to deceive, if possible, even the elect."*

The deceptions are going to look so much like the truth, that if it were possible, true brothers and sisters will be deceived. But look what He says in the next verse. "See, I have told you beforehand." We have been warned. We know what to expect so, therefore we can remain faithful and not follow what is false.

"Therefore we also, since we are surrounded by so great a cloud of witnesses, let us lay aside every weight, and the sin which so easily ensnares us, and let us run with endurance the race that is set before us, looking unto Jesus, the author and finisher of our faith, who for the joy that was set before Him endured the cross, despising the shame, and has sat down at the right hand of the throne of God." Hebrews 12:1, 2

      Let us look only to Christ who is the Author and Finisher of our faith. John warns us about the antichrist not because we do not know the truth, but because we do. He, out of love, is warning us against following the lies that look like the truth. He is reminding us of our anointing from the Holy Spirit. Look at verse 20, "But you have an anointing from the Holy One, and you know all things." We know what we need to know to live in this world because we have the Holy Spirit. That is encouraging for the believer. We don't walk in this dark world alone. We have the Holy Spirit guiding us. We have God's Word. The psalmist says in Psalm 119:105,

"Your word is a lamp to my feet and a light to my path."

1. What spiritual maturity group is John speaking to here? Why?

2. What does it mean that it is the last hour?

3. Is the last hour here yet?

4. What will come in the last hour to deceive? Have some already come?

5. What does Jesus say of Antichrists in Matthew 24:24?

6. Are you prepared to stand against false teachings? How can you further prepare yourself?

7. What do we have that helps us know all that we need to know to stand against false teachings?

8. Find three passages that speak of the Holy Spirit's work in our lives.

9. Do we walk through this dark world alone?

10. How does the fact that the Lord guides and leads you comfort you?

Abide in the Truth

Look at verse 24, "Therefore let that abide in you which you heard from the beginning. If what you heard from the beginning abides in you, you also will abide in the Son and in the Father." Let us abide, live according to, the Father and the Son. We will know that we are abiding in the Father and the Son if we are abiding in the truth that we have heard from the beginning. If we abide in the truth, then we abide in the Son. We have a reward for abiding in the Son. Notice verse 25, "And this is the promise that He has promised us—eternal life." We have been promised and guaranteed eternal life. When we abide in the Son, we have the hope and the promise of eternal life. It is encouraging that amidst the problems of the world and the struggles here in this life, we have the promise of eternal life. It is important that we are studying this book not because we do not know the truth, but because we do know it and therefore must remain fast in it among those who try to deceive us. Look at verse 26, 27 "These things I have written to you **concerning those who try to deceive you**. But the anointing which you have received from Him abides in you, and you do not need that anyone teach you; **but as the same anointing teaches you concerning all things,** and is true, and is not a lie, and just as it has taught you, you will abide in Him." *(emphasis added)* The Holy Spirit teaches us all things and guides us in the truth. Remember what Christ said? This is very similar.

*"But the Helper, the Holy Spirit, whom the Father will send in My name, **He will teach you all things**, and bring to your remembrance all things that I said to you." John 14:26 (emphasis added)*

Notice the last two phrases that were bolded. The same anointing, the Holy Spirit, teaches us concerning all things. The Holy Spirit is our Helper and our Anointing. Let us abide in the

Spirit so that we may know what we need to know and avoid sin. It is my prayer that you know Him. When we know the truth, that is when we will be able to avoid temptation and sin.

1. Why must we abide in that which we have heard?

2. What has God promised to those who believe and abide in Him?

3. What does it mean to abide in the Lord?

4. How does Jesus liken abiding in Him to? (John 15)

5. Do you eagerly await the promise of eternal life?

6. How does this promise comfort you?

Children of our God Part 1

I love the use of words that John picked. He is speaking to His beloved brothers and sisters in a loving and tender way. He writes in such a way that a little child would feel loved and cared for. Look at verse 28, "And now, little children, abide in Him, that when He appears, we may have confidence and not be ashamed before Him at His coming." John lovingly tells us to abide in Christ. With all that has been said about abiding in Him and why we should, John says **now** abide in Him. Take the information that you know and put into practice. We must abide in Him now so that when Christ comes back, we will not be ashamed at His coming, but instead we will have confidence.

Look at verse 29, "If you know that He is righteous, you know that everyone who practices righteousness is born of Him." We have yet another identifier of true Christians. Because God is righteous and because the Spirit is abiding in them, they will be able to live righteously. We will pick up our study in the next chapter and see what kind of love we have been shown and are now therefore children of God. We will also look at sin and how it affects the child of God.

"And now, little children, abide in Him, that when He appears, we may have confidence and not be ashamed before Him at His coming." 1 John 2:28

"The Spirit Himself bears witness with our spirit that we are children of God." Romans 8:16

"Because the creation itself also will be delivered from the bondage of corruption into the glorious liberty of the children of God." Romans 8:21

1. Why must we abide in that which we have heard?

2. What has God promised to those who believe and abide in Him?

3. What does it mean to abide in the Lord?

4. How does Jesus liken abiding in Him to? (John 15)

5. Do you eagerly await the promise of eternal life?

6. How does this promise comfort you?

7. Who teaches all things?

8. Who quickens the heart of people so that they understand God?

9. "But the _____ which you have received from Him _____ in you, and you do not need that anyone teach you; but as the same anointing teaches you concerning ____ things, and is true, and is not a ____, and just as it has taught you, you will _____ in _____." (v.27)

10. What does John mean when he says the truth is not a lie? Isn't that redundant? What point is he trying to prove?

11. Read John 14:26. What truth is Christ telling the disciples that John later states here?

12. How wonderful is it to have the Holy Spirit dwelling in us? Spend time thanking God for the Holy Spirit.

Chapter 3

Children of our God Part 2

I want to start out this chapter by reading the last verse of chapter 2 and the first verse of chapter 3. I do this because that will guide us and give us a good understanding in the transition of chapters. "If you know that He is righteous, you know that everyone who practices righteousness is born of Him. Behold what manner of love the Father has bestowed on us, that we should be called children of God! Therefore the world does not know us, because it did not know Him." The focus here is the Father. If the Father is righteous then His children are righteous. Notice how John has a pattern. He mentions what the Father is and what He does. ("If you know that He is righteous…everyone who practices righteousness is born of Him.") Notice what the Father is and how we are to be in respond to that. That is what the child is to be, one who practices righteousness. Likewise in the next verse, God is our Father and we are His children. We are to behold this great love. Not just observe it or glance over it. We are to observe and contemplate the great love of the Father. We have been shown so much love, that we guilty and stained sinners are. We are children of the Heavenly Father! Don't ignore the greatness of His love. We are children of God and therefore heirs of eternal life. See Romans 8:17,

"And if children, then heirs—heirs of God and joint heirs with Christ."

We are heirs of the gifts and privileges of the Father. Because we are children of God, the world does not know us. Look at the second part of the verse, "Therefore the world does not know us, because it did not know Him." If someone does not know the Father, they do not know the children. We are different from the world. And that's okay because we don't need anything else when we have inherited the riches of the Father. We have the Spirit abiding in us and the Word teaching and encouraging us. We do not need the acceptance of man because we are received by the Father through Christ. I love verse 2, "Beloved, now we are children of God; and it has not yet been revealed what we shall be, but we know that when He is revealed, we shall be like Him, for we shall see Him as He is." Now we are children of God! When Christ comes back to receive us, we will become like Him. We don't know what that will be like fully yet, but we will soon know. We have hope through all of the pain, the suffering of physical and and emotional pain, the persecution, the temptation, and the sin lurking around us, hope of becoming like Him, and free of all of the imperfection here on earth. Hold fast to the hope we have been given! If we have this hope in us and abiding faithfully in it, we will be sanctified and purified as Christ is pure. "And everyone who has this hope in Him purifies himself, just as He is pure." (1 John 3:3) With all that has been said, let us eagerly live in expectation of our Savior who is coming soon!

1. What kind of love has God lavished upon us?

2. What does it mean to be a child of God?

3. Why does the world not know us?

4. What are we going to be like when Christ returns? Will we know the full extent of it?

5. What hope do we have a Christians as found in verse 3?

6. What do those who hope in the Lord strengthen in themselves? (v.3)

The Child of God and Sin

It is important that we understand what lawlessness is. The dictionary says lawlessness is, "A state of disorder due to a disregard of the law." Disorder in our lives is caused by ignoring the law. Disorder never comes from God. Instead God calls us to live orderly lives. 1 Corinthians 14:40 says this,

"Let all things be done decently and in order."

We do this by observing and obeying the law. Now look at verse 3 of our passage, "Whoever commits sin also commits lawlessness, and sin is lawlessness." Sin is disorder. To sin is to disregard God's law which causes disorder and chaos in our lives. Sin causes us to live without peace. When we obey God's law, He blesses us with peace. Look at verses 6-9, "Whoever abides in Him does not sin. Whoever abides in Him does not sin. Whoever sins has neither seen Him nor known Him. Little children, let no one deceive you. He who practices righteousness is righteous, just as He is righteous. He who sins is of the devil, for the devil has sinned from the beginning. For this purpose the Son of God was manifested, that He might destroy the works of the devil. Whoever has been born of God does not sin, for His seed remains in him; and he cannot sin, because he has been born of God." Now we must realize that John here is not talking about occasional sin, but to those who live in sin and do not repent of it. We all sin, but we must not continue in it but turn and repent. Those who do not repent are not of God but of the devil. They walk in darkness. Those who are of Christ cannot be enslaved to sin but will walk in the light.

*"Whoever has been born of God does not sin, for His seed remains in him; and **he cannot sin, because he has been born of God**."*
1 John 3:9 (emphasis added)

1. What is lawlessness?

2. What is the relationship between lawlessness and sin?

3. What does verse 6 mean when it says, "Whoever abides in Him does not sin?"

4. What must we do if we sin?

5. Why was the Son of God manifested according to verse 8?

6. How does this comfort you in your fight against sin and the evil one?

7. Can those who are abiding in God sin? Why or why not?

8. Whose seed remains in a believer? What does this mean?

The Command to Love

Before we get into the command of love, I want to look at verse 10. "In this the children of God and the children of the devil are manifest: Whoever does not practice righteousness is not of God, nor is he who does not love his brother." We know what the child of God looks like and we know what the child of the devil looks like. Their works show what kind of children they really are. He who does not love his brother or practice righteousness is not of God but is of the devil. But those who are of God have a calling to love one another. Verse 11 says, "For this is the message that you heard from the beginning, that we should love one another." We have been given this since from the beginning, but what does John want us to do? Well, John says in his gospel in John 15:13,

"Greater love has no one than this, than to lay down one's life for his friends."

Loving someone requires devotion to him or her. It means complete devotion, even giving your life for him. We are able to show this love because of the love shown to us. While we were still sinners, Christ laid down His life that we may be called a child of God. Now we are called to show this same kind of love to one another. John also provides the way we are not to love. See verse 12, "Not as Cain who was of the wicked one and murdered his brother. And why did he murder him? Because his works were evil and his brother's righteous." We are not to murder our brothers, but we are to look after and protect our brothers and sisters. We are not to be selfish. We are different than the world. The world does not think it is a necessity for us to love. The world thinks that as long as we are happy, anything goes. So John says this in verse 13 and 14 "Do not marvel, my brethren, if the world hates you. We know that we have passed from death to life, because we love the brethren. He who does not love his brother abides in death." The world hates us because we do not live the way they do. The world wants no laws, but we are not like this. We have the command to love and because of the Holy Spirit in us we are **able** to love. Look at verse 15. Look at John's understanding of Christ's statement of love, "Whoever hates his brother is a murderer, and you know that no murderer has eternal life abiding in him." Now look at Matthew 5:21-22,

> *"You have heard that it was said to those of old, 'You shall not murder, and whoever murders will be in danger of the judgment.' But I say to you that whoever is angry with his brother without a cause shall be in danger of the judgment. And whoever says to his brother, 'Raca!' shall be in danger of the council. But whoever says, 'You fool!' shall be in danger of hell fire."*

We know that murderers will not enter eternal life and no one who murders in his heart will enter eternal life. Let us love our brother more and more and by doing so we will walk in the light as He is in the light.

1. How do we know the difference between children of God and children of the devil?

2. What example does John give to show us how to love?

3. Verse 13 states the world's hate of God's people. Why do they hate us?

4. How important is it that love is evident in our lives?

5. Verse 15 speaks of hate being equivalent to murder. Where else in the Bible is this mentioned?

6. How can you love those around you today?

The Manifestation of Love

What does the outworking of love mean? Well, by outworking John means the result of love. It is the fruit of love. Look at verse 16, "By this we know love, because He laid down His life for us. And we also ought to lay down our lives for the brethren." We know love because Christ laid down His life for us. Love was shown. Think back to the section on the imperative of love. We know what love is by the evidence of fruit. And since Christ laid down His life for us and gave us an example of what love is, we should do the same. Our lives should be that of service. We should always be seeking to further benefit our brothers and sisters' lives. Verse 17 gives us a practical way of doing so. "But whoever has this world's goods, and sees his brother in need, and shuts up his heart from him, how does the love of God abide in him?" Our earthly possessions should not be used for ourselves. If we have the resources to help our brother, yet close our hearts, and become selfish, the love of God cannot abide in us. We cannot have the love of God in us. It cannot even be in us if we are selfish. Love is shown by our deeds not just our words. Our words do not mean anything if our actions do not line up with them. Verse 18 backs this up. "My little children, let us not love in word or in tongue, but in deed and in truth." When we love in deed and in truth, that is when the outworking of love is seen. Skipping ahead to verse 23. "And this is His commandment: that we should believe on the name of His Son Jesus Christ and love one another, as He gave us commandment." We are to believe God and follow His Son. It's hard to love one another sometimes, but remember we have been given the Holy Spirit who guides us help us always.

1. What is true love?

2. Is your love this deep?

3. What are we to do with the earthly possessions we have been given?

4. Does God's love abide in those who are selfish and stingy?

5. How can you share the love of God with your possessions?

6. Look at Acts 20:35. How does this relate?

Discerning the Spirit of Truth and the Spirit of Error Part 1

"Now he who keeps His commandments abides in Him, and He in him. And by this we know that He abides in us, by the Spirit whom He has given us." Verse 24 closes off the chapter very well. It summarizes all that we have learned. We know if we are abiding in Him by the Spirit who is in us. If we are bearing the fruits of the Spirit then we have the Spirit of Truth in us. Any other spirit which is not of God is a spirit of error. If we are not bearing good fruits then the Spirit of Truth is not in us. We will go into deeper detail in the next chapter. We, as children of God, have the great privilege to share eternal life with our Father because of Christ's work on this earth. Let us hold fast to this confession.

"But the fruit of the Spirit is love, joy, peace, longsuffering, kindness, goodness, faithfulness, gentleness, self-control. Against such there is no law." Galatians 5:22,23

"For you were once darkness, but now you are light in the Lord. Walk as children of light (for the fruit of the Spirit is in all goodness, righteousness, and truth), finding out what is acceptable to the Lord. And have no fellowship with the unfruitful works of darkness, but rather expose them." Ephesians 5:8-11

1. Is love found in our words alone or is it evidenced our actions?

2. "My little _____, let us not love in word or in tongue, but in _____ and in _____." (v. 18)

3. How does this comfort those whose hearts are condemning them?

4. Do you find that your heart condemns you? What must you remember?

5. "And _____ we ask we _____ from Him, because we _____ His commandments and do those things that are _____ in His sight." (v.22)

6. Does this mean that the Lord will give us anything and everything we ask of Him? Why or why not?

7. What is the commandment that John talks about verse 22? (v.23)

8. How do we know if God abides in us?

Chapter 4

Discerning the Spirit of Truth and the Spirit of Error Pt. 2

"Beloved, do not believe every spirit, but test the spirits, whether they are of God; because many false prophets have gone out into the world." (1 John 4:1) Believer, do not assume every spirit is of God. John warns us of this because Satan will disguise himself to look like the truth and deceive us. Look at 2 Corinthians 11:13-14, and keep notice of the false apostles and what they do.

"For such are false apostles, deceitful workers, transforming themselves into apostles of Christ. And no wonder! For Satan himself transforms himself into an angel of light."

Satan disguises himself as a worker of good. Satan transforms himself into an angel of light, and it is no wonder that others will be deceived. We must be careful that we are not following spirits that are trying to deceive us. We must test them. How? Well the Spirit of God will first bring to our remembrance what Christ has taught us. John 14:26 says,

"But the Helper, the Holy Spirit, whom the Father will send in My name, He will teach you all things, and bring to your remembrance all things that I said to you."

The Holy Spirit will guide us in the truth. He helps us follow Christ more faithfully. Look what verse 2 and 3 says, "By this you know the Spirit of God: Every spirit that confesses that Jesus Christ has come in the flesh is of God, and every spirit that does not confess that Jesus Christ has come in the flesh is not of God. And this is the spirit of the Antichrist, which you have heard was coming, and is now already in the world." We know know how to distinguish between the Spirit of God and of error (or Satan). Because we are in Christ, we have overcome those who are in the world and are trying to deceive us. I love how John assures the believers. Notice his tender tone and his comfort to the children of God by the Truth. "You are of God, little children, and have overcome them, because He who is in you is greater than he who is in the world. They are of the world. Therefore they speak as of the world, and the world hears them. We are of God. He who knows God hears us; he who is not of God does not hear us. By this we know the spirit of truth and the spirit of error." Take comfort in the Father. Take comfort in the Holy Spirit dwelling in you. The Spirit of God is greater than he who is in the world. The battle is already won in Jesus Christ.

"We are of God. He who knows God hears us; he who is not of God does not hear us. By this we know the spirit of truth and the spirit of error."
1 John 4:6

1. Does every spirit come from God?

2. How do we know if a spirt is of God?

3. What kind of spirit is John warning the church about?

4. What test shows whether a spirit is of God or not?

5. Why is it important that we are not believing everything we hear?

6. Those who are of God have overcome what kind of spirits? (v.3)

7. How is it that we have we overcome them?

8. Who is greater, God or the world? What comfort does this bring?

9. How does knowing that God is greater than sin and the world encourage you in your fight against sin? Who has ultimately won the battle?

10. Satan will try to deceive us by twisting the truth. Read 1 Peter 5:8. What must we do to avoid deception?

Knowing God Through Love

We can know God through looking at true love. Ponder verse 7, "Beloved, let us love one another, for love is of God; and everyone who loves is born of God and knows God." Love is an attribute of God. We are to love because God is love. We love because God is love. If we do not love others, we cannot know God. That is an amazing statement. God is so full of love that if it is not in us, we cannot know Him. Look at verse 8, "He who does not love does not know God, for God is love." Verses 9-11 show us that it is not we who loved first, but God. "In this the love of God was manifested toward us, that God has sent His only begotten Son into the world, that we might live through Him. In this is love, not that we loved God, but that He loved us and sent His Son to be the propitiation for our sins. Beloved, if God so loved us, we also ought to love one another." God showed us His love by sending His Son to die on the cross for our sins. He became the payment and sacrifice for the debt we owed. Therefore as redeemed children, we have the calling to love others as Christ has loved us. Let us live in thankfulness for the gift of salvation and love as Christ has loved us.

1. What attribute of God is John talking about here?

2. Why are we to love one another?

3. Why can we love others? (Look ahead to 1 John 4:19)

4. How did God show His love toward us?

5. Do you know and believe the Gospel? Can a true Christian live apart from Christ?

6. God loved us. How must we respond?

7. Can one abide in God and not love others?

Seeing God Through Love

We can know God through love, but we can also see God through love. Look at verse 12. "No one has seen God at any time. If we love one another, God abides in us, and His love has been perfected in us." Although we cannot see God, we can know that He is abiding in us because He is love, and His love is made perfect in us. If we are abiding in Him, His Spirit is in us. And we have assurance in Him. Verse 13 tells us this, "By this we know that we abide in Him, and He in us, because He has given us of His Spirit." If we have His Spirit in us we know that we are abiding in Him and He in us. We also know if we have the Father abiding in us if we confess Jesus Christ. Look at verses 14-16, "And we have seen and testify that the Father has sent the Son as Savior of the world. Whoever confesses that Jesus is the Son of God, God abides in him, and he in God. And we have known and believed the love that God has for us. God is love, and he who abides in love abides in God, and God in him." If we believe the Father sent the Son and that Jesus is God's Son, then that person abides in God and God in Him. Those who believe the gospel abide in Him, and they will walk in the light. Those who believe the love of the Father abide in love, and since God is love those who abide in His love abide in Him. So although no one has ever physically seen God, one can see Him through abiding in Him and walking in the light. Those who are abiding in the *love* of God can have assurance of abiding in God and walking in the light.

"Whoever confesses that Jesus is the Son of God, God abides in him, and he in God." 1 John 4:15

1. Even though we cannot see God, how do we know if God abides in us?

2. When we love others, "His _____ has been _____ in us." (v.12)

3. What must you believe in order for God to abide in you?

4. "God is _____, and he who _____ in love _____ in God, and God in _____." (v.16b)

5. Reflect on these verses. Are you living them out in your life? Are you a person who loves others?

The Completion of Love

John shows us how the love of God is finalized or completed in us. This is what a consummation is. Look at verse 17, "Love has been perfected among us in this: that we may have boldness in the day of judgment; because as He is, so are we in this world." The love of the Father has been perfected in us so that we may be able to have boldness and confidence of eternal life at the coming of Christ and judgement. We have assurance of our salvation because God's love has been given to us and made whole in us. There is nothing to fear in the judgment because God's love drives away fear. "There is no fear in love; but perfect love casts out fear, because fear involves torment. But he who fears has not been made perfect in love." God's perfect love has cast out the fear of judgement and condemnation. Let us abide in the love of the Father that we may not fear. We have the Spirit of God now. Look at 2 Timothy 1:7.

"For God has not given us a spirit of fear, but of power and of love and of a sound mind."

God has given His children a Spirit of power and love and a sound mind. Those who are full of God's Spirit have love and not fear. They have power and not fear. They have a sound mind and not fear. The Spirit of God has driven away the fear in us, and has filled us with the assurance of our salvation in Christ.

"We love Him because He first loved us." 1 John 4:19

1. When God's love is perfected in us, how will we appear on the day of judgement?

2. What is meant by boldness? What can we be bold in?

3. What should we strive to be like according to v. 17b?

4. How can you be more like Jesus in your daily life?

5. Do we have anything to fear if we are abiding in God's love?

6. What type of fear is John speaking about in these verses?

7. Why do we love God?

8. Can anyone love God without being loved by God first?

9. What does this tell you about your salvation?

Obedience by Our Faith Part 1

If we walk in the light we will love our brother. Look at verse 20, "If someone says, "I love God," and hates his brother, he is a liar; for he who does not love his brother whom he has seen, how can he love God whom he has not seen?" We cannot love God, whom we have not seen, unless we love our brother, whom we have seen. John is showing us here that unless we live out what we say, our words do not mean anything. It doesn't mean anything to **say** we love God and then **live** a different way. When I read this section I immediately thought of James chapter 2:24,

"You see then that a man is justified by works, and not by faith only."

Our works show us and others if we have genuine faith. If the love of our brother is not present in us, then we are not truly abiding in the light and can definitely not love God. Therefore if we are of God, we **must** love our brother. Look at how John says it in verse 21. "And this commandment we have from Him: that he who loves God *must* love his brother also." If love is present among the fellow believers of Christ, than it we can truly love God and abide in the light. Let us strive to love our brothers and sisters and so obey the commandment from the Father.

"Thus also faith by itself, if it does not have works, is dead."
James 2:17

1. Go back through the book of 1 John and count how many references are made to loving others.

2. "He who _____ God must _____ his _____ also." (v.21)

3. Why has John brought this up so many times?

Chapter 5

Obedience by Our Faith Part 2

"Whoever believes that Jesus is the Christ is born of God, and everyone who loves Him who begot also loves him who is begotten of Him. By this we know that we love the children of God, when we love God and keep His commandments. For this is the love of God, that we keep His commandments. His commandments are not burdensome. For whatever is born of God overcomes the world. And this is the victory that has overcome the world—our faith. Who is he who overcomes the world, but he who believes that Jesus is the Son of God?" Loving God and each other are tied closely together. Loving God also shows us that we are loving our brother and sister in Christ. We know we are loving God when we obey His commandments. If we are not obeying, then we are just lying to ourselves and everyone else. We, who are of God, have been given a special gift. Our faith allows us to overcome the world. We have been given the victory over sin because of redemption in Christ. Those who believe in Christ have overcome the world. What an encouragement! We are not enslaved to the sins and temptations of the world. We have overcome the world in Christ. Praise God!

1. What relationship is John speaking of here between God and Christ?

2. Can one love God and not Christ or vise versa?

3. How do we know if we have love for God's people?

4. Are the commandments God gave us too difficult that we cannot do them?

5. What does it mean to overcome the world?

6. How is the victory won?

7. Who overcomes the world?

8. How does this help you in your fight against sin and temptation in this world?

Knowing God's Witness is for Sure

Starting at verse 6 we read this, "This is He who came by water and blood—Jesus Christ; not only by water, but by water and blood. And it is the Spirit who bears witness, because the Spirit is truth." To understand this, look at John 19:34.

"But one of the soldiers pierced His side with a spear, and immediately blood and water came out."

What John is probably referring to is the Holy Spirit bearing witness to the Son's incarnation. The Reformation Study Bible comments, "In John's gospel, the testimony God bears to

Jesus His Son is a key theme. The blood and water that flowed from Jesus' side after His death attested to the reality of His death; the wound later confirmed the reality of His resurrection. The Spirit 'bears witness' to the truth of Jesus' incarnation as the divine Christ." John wants his readers to know that it is the Holy Spirit, the Spirit of truth, that bears witness to Christ.

John also speaks of witnesses of the Trinity. The Trinity, who is one, all bear witness together and are one, and the witness of God is greater than that of man. When we believe in God we have been given the witness of the Son's incarnation as well. We have been given the witness of the gospel and are given eternal life in Christ.

"These things I have written to you who believe in the name of the Son of God, that you may know that you have eternal life, and that you may continue to believe in the name of the Son of God."
1 John 5:13

1. What does it mean that Christ came by water and blood? (Look at John 19:34)

2. What is the significance of the Spirit bearing witness to this?

3. What three witnesses are there in heaven? Are they separate from each other?

4. What three witnesses are there on earth?

5. Can we have eternal life apart from Christ?

6. Can we earn any of our salvation? (Ephesians 1:1-20)

7. John writes this letter for two reasons. What are they according to verse 13?

Confidence and Compassion in Our Prayers

As John comes closer to the end of his book, He addresses the topic of prayer. Let's look at verses 14,15 "Now this is the confidence that we have in Him, that if we ask anything according to His will, He hears us. And if we know that He hears us, whatever we ask, we know that we have the petitions that we have asked of Him." We have **confidence** in Him that when we pray He hears us. He will always hear us when we pray. When we pray according to His will and not of our own selfish desires, we can be sure that He hears us and that whatever we asked has been given to us. As children of God, when we ask things according to His will we have the gift of knowing that He hears us and answers us. Matthew 7:11 says,

"If you then, being evil, know how to give good gifts to your children, how much more will your Father who is in heaven give good things to those who ask Him!"

Our Father gives good things to those who ask of Him. Let us be a people of prayer and rest assured that our prayers are heard and answered. John also addresses the issue of a brother in sin.

Look at verse 16,17. "If anyone sees his brother sinning a sin which does not lead to death, he will ask, and He will give him life for those who commit sin not leading to death. There is sin leading to death. I do not say that he should pray about that. All unrighteousness is sin, and there is sin not leading to death." The sin that John is talking about here is likely the sin of refusal to accept the gospel. The sin of unbelief. God forgives those who have repented and turned from their unbelief, but those who refuse His gift of salvation will not go unpunished. My prayer is that we do not walk in darkness and think that we are in the light. God promises salvation and eternal life to any who repent and believe in His Son.

"Seek the Lord while He may be found, Call upon Him while He is near." Isaiah 55:6

1. What confidence do we have in God? How does this correlate with Hebrews 4:16?

2. God _____ us when we pray and he _____ us the things we ask that are according to His will.

3. What does John mean when he says that one sin leads to death and others do not lead to death?

4. What is the sin that leads to death?

Knowing the Truth and Leaving Behind the False

As John comes to the end of his book to the believers, he wants His readers to know the true and reject the false. Look at verses 18-21. "We know that whoever is born of God does not sin; but he who has been born of God keeps himself, and the wicked one does not touch him. We know that we are of God, and the whole world lies under the sway of the wicked one. And we know that the Son of God has come and has given us an understanding, that we may know Him who is true; and we are in Him who is true, in His Son Jesus Christ. This is the true God and eternal life. Little children, keep yourselves from idols. Amen." We know that those who are of God are protected from the evil one and is no longer enslaved to the sin in the world. We know that the Son has come and has redeemed us and therefore has given us a knowledge of the Father who is true. The last words John wrote were "keep yourselves from idols. Amen." Children of God, in all that we have learned in the past 5 chapters, hold fast to it, and do not turn away to idols. Those who hold firm to the end will receive the crown of life. Let us run the race set before us not turning away to idols. Be encouraged in the truth!

"Let us hold fast the confession of our hope without wavering, for He who promised is faithful." Hebrews 10:23

"But Christ as a Son over His own house, whose house we are if we hold fast the confidence and the rejoicing of the hope firm to the end." Hebrews 3:6

1. Can Satan touch those who belong to God?

2. What is John's last command to the church?

3. Why would he end the letter in this way?

4. Are there things in your life that you hold closer than God?

Here we are at the end of John's first letter to the Christian church. Let us desire to live out all that we have learned in this book. Keep pressing into Christ. Flee from sin.

> *"See what kind of love the Father has given to us, that we should be called children of God; and so we are. The reason why the world does not know us is that it did not know him. Beloved, we are God's children now, and what we will be has not yet appeared; but we know that when he appears we shall be like him, because we shall see him as he is. And everyone who thus hopes in him purifies himself as he is pure." (1 John 3:1-3)*

We belong to God. We are His children. Take what you have learned and put it into practice. Trust in Him and continue to abide in God and His love.

> *"By this we know love, because He laid down His life for us. And we also ought to lay down our lives for the brethren."*
> *1 John 3:16-17*

Made in the USA
Lexington, KY
31 January 2018